Hooks!

The Invisible Sales Superpower

Create Network
Marketing Prospects
Who Want to Know More

KEITH & TOM "BIG AL" SCHREITER

Hooks! The Invisible Sales Superpower

© 2021 by Keith & Tom "Big Al" Schreiter

Published by Fortune Network Publishing

PO Box 890084

Houston, TX 77289 USA

Telephone: +1 (281) 280-9800

BigAlBooks.com

ISBN-13: 978-1-956171-05-1

CONTENTS

PREFACE

How we start determines how we end. First impressions are important.

Our future success depends on a few seconds of first impression.

And it gets worse!

Humans make final decisions in seconds. With limited time, humans sort out uninteresting conversations immediately. They prejudge, use heuristics, and have salesman avoidance programs. Why do humans judge what we say so harshly?

They do this so that they have more time to think about what is important to them. They want their problems solved. They want entertainment. And our ordinary messages won't make the cut.

Think about an evening of mindless scrolling through social media on our phones. We start watching a viral video clip. It moves slowly and doesn't capture our interest. How long does it take for us to scroll to another video clip? Seconds.

Or imagine that we open a shop on a busy street. We darken the windows and door to our shop. No one can see in. Even if we have the best bargains in the universe, no one will know. They will pass by our shop. If we don't hook the people walking past our shop, nothing happens.

To get our prospects' attention, we must hook their interest within the opening seconds of our message. Can we do it? Can we compete with social media? Compete with their passions? Compete with their problems? Compete with their current thoughts?

If we can't, our conversations go nowhere. We talk, but our prospects aren't home. Their minds are busy thinking about other things. They hear what we say as muffled background noise. Our attempt at communication fails.

The greatest sales message in the world is useless if no one is listening. Our job? To hook our prospects' attention. We want our prospects to think, "I want to know more."

Boring and predictable opening sentences fail. But don't worry! We can create awesome opening hooks that will separate us from our competition. To do this, we won't have to be creative geniuses. It is easier than that.

This book has templates and examples of effective opening hooks that we can modify for our use. Inspiration awaits!

THE BIG SECRET.

A distributor with a victim mindset says: "Nobody wants to hear about my business!"

The professional says: "Oh. Nobody? Are you sure?"

The distributor says: "Nobody will even make an appointment. This business doesn't work."

The professional says: "Maybe everybody wants to hear about our business. They just don't want to hear it from you!"

The distributor says: "Ouch. That is cold."

An uncomfortable silence follows. Our victim distributor looks down, shuffles his feet, clears his throat.

The distributor says: "Uh, go on. Tell me more."

The professional says: "This might be painful. Can you take it?"

The distributor says: "I either listen and learn ... or quit. I don't want to quit. Bring on the facts."

The professional says: "You invested in designer clothes, great cologne, a streaming subscription, an expensive haircut, and an impressive car. How much did you invest into learning basic magic words?"

The distributor says: "Uh, I haven't learned any magic words. I was busy updating my latest social media profile."

More silence.

> **The distributor rolls his eyes and says:** "Okay. Continue. Tell me more."

> **The professional says:** "Well, did you at least learn the big secret? The one I told you about?"

> **The distributor says:** "The big secret??? You mean there is a big secret that could change my career?"

> **The professional says:** "Of course. The big secret all the pros use. The top level skill that makes prospects beg for presentations, rejection-free. Pros use this all the time. Amateurs never use it. They don't know it."

> **The distributor says:** "Uh, you've probably mentioned this secret before, but this time I will listen. I promise!"

> **The professional says:** "Hooks! Magic words on steroids!"

The distributor twists his face into a giant question mark.

> **The professional says:** "Hooks. The invisible sales super-power that turns amateurs into pros. If we use good hooks, prospects beg us for presentations. If we want success, we need to sell and market at the highest level. And that means using hooks."

> **The distributor says:** "Are hooks like movie trailers that get us to buy tickets to the next movie release?"

> **The professional says:** "Yes, but shorter. Think of the opening sentences to great novels. They hook our interest. We have to know more."

Panic starts to set in.

The distributor cringes and says: "The idea of talking to people terrifies me. What if they are not interested? Won't I feel rejected?"

The professional says: "If you use great hooks to start the conversation, don't worry. They will be interested and ask to know more."

The distributor says: "This is terrifying. I prefer to spend months developing relationships. Then build strong bonds where others will hang on every word I say. And then suddenly, months later, my prospects decide to magically join."

The professional says: "And ..."

The distributor says: "And I haven't had much luck with that approach either. But I don't want to change my introverted ways."

The professional says: "Stay introverted. Use hooks. Then only talk to the people who beg you for more information."

And so the conversation continued. The distributor learned that he didn't have this sales superpower ... yet. But guess what he will be learning next.

WHAT CHOICE WILL WE MAKE?

"I arrived late for work, sat at my desk, and felt the death stare from my demonic boss burn the back of my head. I knew it was Doomsday."

Our prospect listens and thinks, "Ouch. This isn't going to end well."

We continue, "It was at that moment, I decided to grow up and work to become my own boss. That is why I started my business."

Message delivered. Our prospect felt the danger, and mentally lived the scene with us.

Or we could have just said, "I wanted to quit my job."

Which opening is more interesting to our prospects? Which opening will hook our prospects' attention? The answer is obvious.

Another example of a hook opening?

"My mother-in-law is germaphobic. Last week I was stuck in a car with her, and I started having an allergy-induced sneezing attack. But I have the 'eye of the tiger,' so I started to tell her about my business opportunity. I live for danger."

Yeah, we want to know what comes next.

If our prospects scroll through their phones while we talk, the end of our career is near. Prospects are worried about mortgage payments, job stress, and family situations. We need to be more interesting than their personal problems.

How about another example?

"Six months ago, I turned ... 40. I took off my makeup, stared into the mirror, and stuck my finger inside my biggest facial wrinkle. I asked myself, 'Is it possible to heal wrinkles from the inside?'"

We want to know the answer.

Bad hooks.

Now, we would never say anything like the following openings from the 1960s pyramid scheme days. But maybe we've heard these openings from other networkers before:

- "My name is ..."
- "Let me tell you about ..."
- "Our product's quality is ..."
- "Here is the link to the company video ..."
- "I just need a few minutes of your time ..."
- "Do you keep your income options open ..."
- "This is a ground-floor opportunity ..."
- "Unlimited financial opportunity ..."
- "Our unique formula ..."

Ugh, and it gets worse.

- "Our proprietary blockchain algorithm ..."
- "We have an award-winning scientist ..."
- "Let me explain residual income ..."

Stop! This is painful to read.

There is a huge difference between a good opening hook and a bad opening hook. How about a little test?

Which opening strategy is better?

> 1. Get our prospects to engage with us and beg us to continue? Or,
>
> 2. Set off their salesman alarms?

If we don't know how to create interesting hooks, then we get sentenced to a career of setting off salesman alarms.

Do these hooks feel any better?

- "I was thinking things are looking up, and then 15 seconds later, I got fired!"
- "I arrived at work on Monday morning, and the entire office was empty. No furniture. No people."
- "My doctor said, 'Show me your hands. I want to check for dirt under your fingernails since you insist on digging your own grave.'"
- "My four-year-old daughter said, 'Daddy, if you don't like your job, why do you keep going there?'"
- "When I got my annual profit-sharing bonus from work, and it was only $29, I knew something had to change."
- "Everyone gets bills. But not everyone has to pay those bills. I never knew this."

So what exactly is the definition of a hook?

We can think of a hook as a first sentence or ice breaker … on steroids.

Hooks make others wonder, "What comes next? Tell me more." Curiosity creates interest. And if our prospects are interested in what we say next, then they will hear our message.

Let's start now.

CAN WE SPOT THE RIGHT ANSWER?

Which of these two messages hooks our prospects' attention better?

Message #1: "Amazing breakthrough formula for diet and weight loss!"

Message #2: "My chubby cat found a better solution to my weight problem."

Message #1 warns prospects that a commercial is coming.

Message #2 makes our prospects want to know more.

Did we pick the right answer?

If we picked message #1, we are salespeople.

If we picked message #2, we are **effective** salespeople. Prospects beg to know more. We don't worry about rejection. Every opening in our appointment calendar is filled with a prospect waiting for us.

Both messages target prospects who want to lose weight.

But message #2 hooks their interest and curiosity.

It feels more like a story and takes away the feeling of an impending high-pressure sales pitch.

This works even better with cold prospects. Cold prospects hate hard-core commercials. Our cold prospects don't know about our weight-loss problem, our weight-loss journey, or any of our challenges and frustrations. They don't even know how good our original solution was. Message #2 signals the beginning of a story. Our prospects naturally want to know our story.

Can we start the story in a different way?

"Hiding the sugar from me was my family's first mistake."

This sentence feels like a story. We introduce the situation (hiding the sugar from me) and the plot (our family's first mistake).

Notice how the sentence is short and clear. Our prospects don't feel like this is the beginning of a commercial. They want to know what the second mistake could be.

As long as we are using a weight-loss example, let's come up with a few more hook openings.

- "The smell of cupcakes was the last thing I remembered before passing out."
- "Hoarding food is a national sport for our family. I decided to change the rules."
- "I gained more weight. And I gained more weight. And then, the tsunami started."
- "Drooling at the smell of peanut butter was my first hint."
- "The sugar fairy was dead. And the ghostly look of the pizza delivery boy was creepy."

Enough with the dieters. Let's expand this with more examples.

- "Do bacon-flavored brochures unfairly influence travelers?"

- "My high school 40th reunion featured creatures from the wastelands. What happened to the classmates I remembered?"
- "I didn't know my new boss was a unionized vampire."
- "Why did my new co-workers have two puncture marks on their necks?"
- "My career ends on Thursday. Was I my worst enemy?"
- "When our travel agent gets us a bargain seaside view, what is the first question we should ask?"
- "It took only two days before my new office mates started to act strange."
- "My daughter wondered why I never went to work anymore."
- "My neighbor refused to look at me relaxing in my lawn chair as he left for work."

These hooks make prospects ask, "What comes next?"

If there is no interest, our conversation goes no further. Engaging our prospects makes the rest of our conversation easy.

What happens when we don't engage our prospects? They stare blankly into space. Our voice goes up in pitch as we panic, but we still have a boring message. We have to fix our message. Talking louder won't fix our problem.

Creating hooks will be fun.

You might be thinking, "I am not a creative genius. How will I come up with interesting hooks for my prospects?"

No worries. This will be easier than you think.

THE UNEXPECTED HOOK.

Remember these two messages from the last chapter?

- "Amazing breakthrough formula for diet and weight loss!"
- "My chubby cat found a better solution to my weight problem."

Message #2 is more interesting.

Why? Because we don't expect a chubby cat to solve weight-loss challenges.

Let's take a closer look at our prospect's reaction to these messages.

Message #1: "Amazing, breakthrough formula for diet and weight loss!"

Prospect's reaction: "Whoa! Sales pitch coming. This is going to be a commercial. I need to shield myself from incoming sales-man hype. Everything is amazing according to salespeople."

Message #2: "My chubby cat found a better solution to my weight problem."

Prospect's reaction: "Huh? What? Tell me more. How can a chubby cat find a solution? This is interesting. Tell me what happened."

What is going on in our prospects' brains when we use an unexpected hook?

Let's take a quick look at the human brain.

The #1 purpose of the human brain is to keep us alive. Our brains run automatic survival programs full-time.

One of these survival programs is prediction. Our brain tries to predict what comes next. We don't want any surprises. Surprises might get us killed.

Take a little walk. Our brain will ignore the birds, the cars, and the wind, thinking, "Yeah. I have seen this all before. This is normal. I know what is coming next."

But what if something unusual or unexpected happens, like an earthquake? The ground shakes. Our brains think, "Yikes! Look out. Don't fall. Make sure something doesn't fall on us. Be careful!"

Our brain didn't expect the ground to shake. Now our brain's focus is entirely on the ground movement. We are at full alert. Our attention is 100% on the moving ground.

So if our message has an unexpected ending, wow! We have our prospect's full attention. Isn't that what we want? Someone listening to what we have to say?

Instant creativity.

Here is an easy two-step formula to create unlimited unexpected hooks.

Step #1: Think of a great benefit we want our prospects to pay attention to. This could be about our business opportunity, our products, or our services.

Step #2: Put this benefit into an unexpected setting. Ask ourselves, "Where wouldn't I expect this benefit?"

Now, let's take a look at our original weight-loss example.

"My chubby cat found a better solution to my weight problem."

Yep. Associating a chubby cat with a weight-loss discovery is shocking to the brain. The brain doesn't expect this. Time to pay attention! Let's look at a few more weight-loss examples with unexpected patterns.

- "I thought about entering the Miss Donut Beauty Pageant."
- "Why I put my bathroom scale next to the kitty litter box in the garage."
- "Our diet support group meets at Pizza Hut."
- "Why Dairy Queen hates me."
- "This is why they created the 'French fry' diet."
- "My wife asked me, 'Are you getting a tan from the refrigerator light? Again?'"

How interesting and unexpected can we be? How about this:

"I felt guilty not doing my weekly exercises as I approached the gym. But then, out of the corner of my eye, I saw my personal trainer munching donuts in the parking lot."

Enough about diets. The first three letters in "diet" are depressing. Let's try some other products and services.

Step #1: The benefit. In this case, lower utility bills.

Step #2. Put the benefit into an unexpected setting.

- My doctor told me to lower my stress by getting a less expensive utility provider.
- Why my mother-in-law laughed at my utility bill.
- This is why I tried to teach my cat to turn off the lights.
- I took a basic math test … and failed. (I should have picked the lower bill.)
- My 8-year-old daughter's math class can pick out the best utility provider.
- My spouse and I burned incense before we opened our cellphone bill.
- I asked the emergency room doctor, "How many people come here after opening their utility bill?"

If we can make utility bills interesting with a hook, what else could we try?

Step #1: Benefit. Super-moisturizing skincare.

Step #2. Put the benefit into an unexpected setting.

- I tried the skin windburn test by jumping out of an airplane.
- I put my face to the test against the kindergarten class.
- I just found out where wrinkles go to die.
- My mom tried three different moisturizers before her fire walk.

But what about organic cleaning products? Can't get more boring than that, right?

Step #1: Benefit. Natural, non-toxic cleaning products.

Step #2. Put the benefit into an unexpected setting.

- What our dog uses for toothpaste.
- I asked the emergency room doctor, "How many people come here after cleaning their house?" (See a pattern? Yeah, we don't have to be original.)
- How our goldfish survived our laundry.
- The most deadly laundry detergent on earth.

How about some examples for nutrition?

- My new personal trainer looked at me and said, "Have you considered transplants?"
- I thought Vitamin C was supposed to make you feel better!
- They tested our energy capsule on vampires, and yes, it did keep them up all day.
- My doctor looked up from my cholesterol test and asked, "Do you live in a cheese factory?"
- My doctor's twisted face said it all: "You know, dying young is inconvenient."
- A journey of 1,000 miles starts with a single step ... and usually ends a few minutes later because we don't have the nutritional go-power to make it.

Some examples for opportunity?

- I saw my boss counting his coins at the checkout counter. I wondered, "Will that be me when I finally get promoted?"
- On Friday night, our company had an employee appreciation banquet. They wanted to recognize everyone with ten or more years of service. No one qualified.

- I had a dream about my job last night. Another nightmare. Panic attack.

- They called and offered me the job. I jumped up and down, hugged my spouse, and then went into a deep depression.

- The highlight of my work? Coffee break! Fire drills come in second.

- I begged my supervisor, "Please fire me."

A few more? Let's make them even more unexpected.

- I have no friends. That is why I go to work. Money isn't everything.

- My company laid off fifty percent of us. Horrifying. But it wasn't a problem, since I never showed up anyway.

- The best part of my job is taking sick days. But I used up my allotment for the next seven years.

- I get paid more than my boss, but I still hate my job.

- When they fired me, I felt like an escaped mental patient. Now everyone in the restaurant is staring at me.

- The boss told me, "Of course you're not getting a promotion this year. You know, you are just not smart enough, even for your current job."

- I asked my boss, "So will I keep my job, or be part of the budget cut?" He didn't look up. He kept playing Solitaire on his phone. Silence.

- My dog seems irritated that I don't go to work anymore. Does therapy for dogs exist?

We don't want to be boring and blend into the background. We want to be the voice our prospect hears. We can do this.

So how can we come up with unusual settings for our benefits?

Consider using a thesaurus.

Don't have a thesaurus in our library? No problem.

Thesaurus.com will work fine.

We will want to use the "opposite" of normal. That means we take a word, then look up the opposite. This would naturally be unexpected. Let's do an example.

Our benefit is that we get a monthly bonus. Let's focus on the word "bonus" and go to our thesaurus. We see similar words such as:

Benefit

Bounty

Dividend

Gift

Gratuity

Perk

Premium

Prize

Reward

Commission

Plus

Tip

Additional Compensation

Fringe Benefit

Golden Parachute

Handout

Special Compensation

These are the "expected" words.

Now, let's look at the list of antonyms (words with the opposite meaning) to "bonus."

Disadvantage

Loss

Penalty

Punishment

Any ideas now? Imagine we like the word "penalty." Let's put it to use.

- "No annual bonus checks from the company this year, but they did announce the annual penalty."
- "We don't get bonuses at work. We get penalties."

This is going to be so much fun. Our hooks will ensure our message gets an audience.

Still having trouble coming up with something unexpected? Then, try setting our hooks in an unusual location. Some examples?

- A pig wrestling event.
- A proctologist appointment.
- A dog wedding.
- The nail clippers convention.
- A marshmallow packing plant.
- A clown suit factory.
- A children's petting zoo.

- A squirrel charity banquet.
- An acne workshop.

Some more unexpected hooks?

- I found out why vegans who exercise get so many heart attacks.
- I didn't know that commuting to work takes 2.3 years off our lives.
- Turns out pimpled high school freshmen have a higher net worth than their parents.
- Turns out dieting makes things worse.
- Why mothers have better-looking skin than their daughters.
- How calling in sick helps us get raises.

Let's end this chapter with a few more unexpected hook examples.

- "I saw my banker making sandwiches at Subway. Should I take financial advice from him?"
- "My ex-banker said to me, 'Welcome to Walmart.'"
- "Dairy Queen declined my debit card."
- "I just finished my morning affirmations when my boss called and fired me."

Anyone can create unexpected hooks. We don't need many. We don't have to create a new one every day. All we need to do is to take a bit of time, create a few of these unexpected hooks, and see which ones get the best response.

THE QUESTION HOOK.

Why do we use hooks? To engage our prospects. To take our prospects' minds away from their phones and current thoughts, and compel them to listen to our message.

Questions create automatic engagement. Our subconscious minds have programs that make us search for answers. The "unknown" attracts us.

Our prospects' conscious minds can entertain only one thought at a time. We want that thought to be about our message.

When prospects hear a question, they stop what they are thinking, pay attention to the question, and then think about how they will reply. This is a built-in human response.

To trigger this response, we need to make sure our questions are interesting, create curiosity, and beg for an answer. Let's warm up our thinking muscles. Here are some questions we can ask prospects. These questions get our prospects to wonder, "What happens next?"

- "Why do you think so many people quit their jobs when offered a big promotion and a pay raise?"
- "Do you know why most airline pilots have part-time businesses?"
- "Can you guess the three best fat-burning foods?"
- "Ever wonder why wrinkles start on our foreheads first?"

- "If you had a part-time side hustle that equaled one day's pay, would you switch to a four-day workweek, or do something else with the extra money?"
- "I wondered why I was calling in sick five times a week."
- "Can full-time losers make it big in a part-time business?"
- "Is a full-time job the best way for us to make a living?"

Simple questions. Instant engagement. It's easy to see how hooks get the interest of our prospects. Let's look at more examples and imagine what our prospects might think.

- "What do you think of the success plan they gave us in school?" (Our prospects might think, "Hey! They didn't give me a success plan! Do you have one?")
- "What is more fun than getting money in the mail?" (Our prospects might think, "You get money in the mail? How does that work?")
- "To get paid what we are worth, how much should we get paid per hour?" (Our prospects might think, "I don't know about you, but I should be getting paid a lot more!")
- "How many weeks of vacation do you need each year?" (Our prospects might think, "No one ever asked me that. Are there options? Let's see. I could use a vacation at least every two months.")
- "Do you swallow hard when the boss asks you to work weekends?" (Our prospects might think, "I have to work at least one day every weekend! It's a requirement. Ugh. Do you have a solution?")
- "If we don't change anything, what do you think our situation will look like next year?" (Our prospects might

think, "About the same. I will be one year older. Still struggling with bills.")

- "Do you know the three biggest mistakes that poor people make?" (Our prospects might think, "Let me think. Hmmm. Not sure. This isn't a good sign. I'd better listen.")

This feels like we can control other people's thoughts. But the truth is that our hooks are more interesting than the current thoughts of our prospects. They choose to engage with us.

Let's try this question hook approach for a few products and services.

- "How much should lawyers charge per hour?" (Our prospects might think, "Oh my. Lawyers are expensive. I wonder if there is a way to get legal help without paying big money?")

- "How many pounds overweight should we be at age 50?" (Our prospects might think, "I don't know. I'd better ask to see if I am bumping the limits.")

- "Would you like to feel healthier if it only took 15 seconds a day?" (Our prospects might think, "That is my maximum time limit. What do I do during those 15 seconds? Tell me more.")

- "Do you know anyone in pain?" (Our prospects might think, "Yes, I do. Do you have some advice or something that can help?")

- "Do you know how much you are paying per kilowatt hour for your electricity?" (Our prospects might think, "Uh, no idea. Probably too much. I don't even know how to check. Looks like you might be an expert on this. Tell me more!")

- "What is the easiest food to eat for quick weight loss?" (Our prospects might think, "These chicken wings and French fries definitely don't qualify. I wonder what that weight-loss food could be? I can't wait to find out.")
- "Do you know why my wrinkles are going away?" (Our prospects might think, "I need to know. My wrinkles are looking like canyons. Help! Tell me now!")
- "How much should we be paying for our phone service?" (Our prospects might think, "I don't know. Hey, that is not good. Maybe I am paying too much.")
- "If we don't take care of our bodies, then who will?" (Our prospects might think, "Ouch. Looks like others have neglected taking care of my body. Time for me to step up. Tell me more.")
- "Could this be the eighth wonder of the world? (Our prospects might think, "What is it?")

Use these questions as prompts, templates, or idea starters for our products and services.

Let others inspire our creativity.

An easy way to get creative for our opportunity, products, and services is to customize the interesting questions we hear others use. Here is an example:

Original question: "How much should lawyers charge per hour?"

Our inspired versions?

- "How much overcharge should we tolerate on our phone bills?"

- "How many wrinkles should we expect at age 40?"
- "How many times a year should we get a raise?"
- "How many toxic chemicals are in one cup of laundry detergent?"
- "How many minutes should it take us to fall asleep at night?"

If we hear a great question, let's write it down. This question can inspire us to make a great customized version for our pros-pects.

Rhetorical questions.

What is a rhetorical question? For our hook purposes, it means we already know the answer. Here is an example.

"Do you get an electric bill?" is a rhetorical question. Of course we know the answer will be, "Yes." This sets up the follow-up question, "Would it be okay if it was lower?"

In two sentences, we've hooked our prospect's mind and executed a quick follow-up that completed our message.

More examples of easy rhetorical questions?

- Do you hate dieting?
- Do you like keeping your skin looking young?
- Do you hate wrinkles?
- Do you think lawyers are expensive?
- Do you hate using toxic chemicals around your home?
- Do you hate putting toothpaste chemicals inside our children's mouths?
- Do you like coffee?

- Do you want to avoid growing old?

- Are you tired of paying big mobile phone bills?

- Do you hate stress?

And how would we follow up after their reply? An easy fill-in-the-blanks formula is:

"Would it be okay if you had an option to ..."

This relieves the pressure of a sales pitch. We simply offer them an option.

But during these few sentences, our prospects are totally focused on our message. Excellent!

Some rhetorical questions for our opportunity?

- Do you hate commuting to work?

- Are you tired of bosses?

- Do you need better working hours?

- Do you want to avoid working weekends?

- Would you like to create your own work schedule?

- How do you feel about raises?

- Would free vacations be more fun?

But what if we want to be more direct, but still avoid rejection?

We could ask ourselves some tough questions. That way our prospects can safely observe from a distance. Don't worry. Prospects will still get the message. They will mentally ask themselves the same question. Some examples?

- "So I asked myself, 'Who makes more money, me or my boss?'"

- "I wondered to myself, 'Why do I gain five pounds every time I diet?'"

- "How could I avoid looking like I graduated from the Clown School of Makeup?"

- "I was thinking, 'How could I avoid wasting my life sitting in traffic?'"

- "When I looked at my paycheck, I thought, 'How could I have been so dumb?'"

- "I wondered, 'Will my wrinkles get larger or smaller?'"

- "I thought, 'Work for 50 weeks. Vacation for two weeks. Is that fair?'"

- "So I am thinking, 'How much is my health worth? $50? $500?'"

- "I cringed and thought, 'I am tired of others taking advantage of me.'"

- "I wondered, 'Can a pill turn fat into muscle?'"

- "I wondered, 'Is taking a 40-hour-a-week job a mistake?'"

Our prospects want to know what comes next. They can't wait for our second sentence.

Question hooks rock.

Can we start with a riddle?

Riddles guarantee engagement. Riddles create curiosity. Prospects must stop what they are doing to come up with an answer.

What is a riddle? A question that may include hints, doubled or veiled meaning, a play on words, mild humor, stupid observations, or just a fun puzzle to solve. Some general examples:

> Q. What two things can we never eat for breakfast?
>
> A. Lunch and dinner.
>
> Q. What do Jack the Ripper and Winnie the Pooh have in common?
>
> A. Their middle names.
>
> Q. Two fathers and two sons are in a car, yet there are only three people in the car. How is this possible?
>
> A. They are grandfather, father, and son.

Riddles can be entertaining, but they are also great at creating curiosity. We want to make sure the riddles are related to our products, services or opportunities.

Now, riddles are not good for ice breakers. Challenging our new contact immediately is a bit antisocial. Save the riddles for later in the conversation.

SIMPLE MAGIC WORDS.

To hook our prospects' attention away from their current thoughts, we don't have to be a genius. Instead, we can memorize a few magic word sequences. A simple example?

"Guess what?"

Say these two words to others, and ta-da!

We have their attention. Their minds think, "Wait. Stop what I am thinking. Let me guess what … uh, wait. I have no idea what to guess. Maybe I should reply, 'I don't know. What?'"

Does this seem too simple? Too general? No problem. We can improve. But remember, we are as little as two words away from hooking someone's attention.

How about a real-life example?

At work, while chatting with a coworker, we say, "Guess what?"

Of course we know the response. Our coworker will always say, "What?"

Now we can deliver our message. We say, "I was feeling discouraged about my future here, so I started a part-time business."

Can we guess the next words from our coworker? "Tell me more."

This simple two-word hook means our coworker will hear our message. That is our goal.

How about a product example?

If we sell nutrition products, at the gym we could say, "Guess what?"

We know our prospect will reply, "What?"

We continue, "I got my workout benefits to last twice as long."

Done.

Services? Let's make this conversation a little longer. It is fun to have some variety.

We say: "You still get your phone bill, right?"

Our friend says: "Yes."

We say: "Guess what?"

Our friend says: "What?"

We say: "There is a good chance we can get a discount."

Done.

Now that we see the power in a simple two-word hook, let's improve on it.

Let's try four words.

"I just found out."

If you have read our previous Big Al books on ice breakers, appointments, and closing, you know how effective these four words are.

The formula is:

"I just found out" + "our benefit."

Some quick examples?

- "I just found out how we can earn more money part-time than our boss does full-time."

- "I just found out how we can start a business with almost no risk."

- "I just found out how to lose weight and keep it off."

- "I just found out why our utilities cost so much."

We get the idea. Let's have fun making up dozens of these easy hooks that get our prospects' attention.

Now let's try nine words.

"There are two types of people in the world."

If someone says to us, "There are two types of people in the world," what do we think? "Two types? I am curious. What are the two types? Which type am I? This might be important for my survival. I'd better pay attention. So ... what are the two types?"

Our prospects forget the personal drama in their minds and totally focus on what we are about to say next.

It's almost too easy.

Some examples?

"There are two types of people in the world:

1. Those who had their dreams sucked out by their vampire, dream-killing employers.

2. Those that still want to do something with their lives."

Any prospect with ambition will want to continue this conversation.

"There are two types of people in the world:

1. Those who pay the maximum taxes out of their paychecks.

2. Those who know how to get tax breaks with a home-based business."

That is a perfect hook for detail-driven personalities like accountants and engineers.

"There are two types of people in the world.

1. Those who are open-minded and looking for opportunity.

2. Those who are closed-minded and willing to accept whatever their bosses will give them."

If we are looking for motivated prospects, this gives them an opportunity to raise their hands.

More opportunity examples?

- "There are two types of people in the world. Those who complain about money, and those who know how to get more."

- "There are two types of people in the world. Those who make monthly car payments, and those who don't. Which group do you want to be in?"

- "There are two types of people in the world. Those who work hard and help their bosses reach their dreams, and those who work hard on their families' dreams."

- "There are three types of people in the world. Those who understand math, and those who don't." (Just had to throw this one in to keep our attention. Be unexpected!)

Don't underestimate the power of these nine words. We can use them to open our prospects' minds before our presentation.

- "There are two types of people in the world. Those who look for reasons why things **can** work, and those who look for reasons why things **won't** work."

Most prospects will naturally want to be in the first group. Now we will have less skepticism and negativity as our conversation continues.

Want it to be even stronger?

- "There are two types of people in the world, those who are open-minded and look for opportunity, and those who have given up on life." (This is a great way to handle resistant prospects.)

This is getting fun. We can use our creativity to include our best benefits as well.

- "There are two types of people in the world, those who get to travel and see the world in person, and those who only see it on television."

- "There are two types of university graduates in the world. Those who want to be their own boss, and those that resign themselves to 45 years of hard labor working for someone else."

Product examples?

- "There are two types of people in the world. Those who eat funny foods, exercise, and starve themselves to lose weight, and those who simply change what they have for breakfast."

- "There are two types of people in the world. Those who use our night cream and make their skin younger while they sleep, and those who wrinkle a little bit more every night."

- "There are two types of people in the world. Those who want to keep their homes safe from chemicals, and those who don't."

- "There are two types of people in the world. Those who get tired every afternoon, and those who have energy all day long."

- "There are two types of grandmothers in the world. Those who have more energy than their little home-wrecking grandchildren, and those who don't."

Service examples?

- "There are two types of people in the world. Those who worry about identity theft, and those who protect themselves from it."

- "There are two types of people in the world. Those who get discounts on their utility bills, and those who pay the full price."

- "There are two types of people in the world. Those who pay full retail for their holidays, and those who take five-star holidays for the price of a budget hotel."

This gets better. When we say there are two types of people in the world, our prospects will choose which group they want to be in. This pre-closes our prospects.

Are these the only nine words that can hook our prospects' attention? Of course not. Let's look at another nine-word hook.

"I have some good news and some bad news."

If you haven't read our previous books, here is the formula.

"I have some good news and some bad news." + "The prospect's problem." + "Our solution."

People generally want to hear the bad news first. Let's do a few quick examples to show the power of this nine-word phrase.

- "I have some good news and some bad news. The bad news is that our utility bills keep going up every year. The good news is that I found out how we can stop this."

- "I have some good news and some bad news. The bad news is that our skin wrinkles a little bit more every night. The good news is that we can stop this."

- "I have some good news and some bad news. The bad news is that we are getting older. The good news is that we can slow this down."

This nine-word phrase is irresistible. Everyone desperately wants to hear what we say next.

"Would you like to know how I did it?"

This magic word formula is easy. We state our benefit. Then ask our prospects if they want to hear more. If they say "yes," well, this gets easy.

Here is the formula.

"Our benefit" + "Would you like to know how I did it?"

Examples?

- "I finally lost those last 15 pounds. Would you like to know how I did it?"
- "Next year I plan to work from home. Would you like to know my plan?"
- "My mother-in-law looks 15 years younger. Would you like to know how she did it?"
- "I finally stopped wrinkling while I slept. Would you like to know how I did it?"
- "My neighbor just became his own boss. Would you like to know how he did it?"
- "I am going to win a free holiday this year. Would you like to know my plan?"

By now, these magic word formulas should feel easy.

Three things ...

Our short-term memory is, well, short. We can only hold so many chunks of information before they start falling off our memory plate.

Humans are able to process information more effectively when it forms a simple pattern. And what is the simplest pattern? A pattern of three.

Some examples of easy-to-remember patterns of three:

- Rock! Paper! Scissors!
- "Three Little Pigs."
- "Three Little Kittens."
- Past, present, and future.
- The Three Stooges.

Three things. Easy to remember and repeat to others.

- "Finger Lickin' Good." - Kentucky Fried Chicken.
- Beginning, middle, and end.
- Faith, hope, and charity.
- "Truth, Justice, and the American Way." - Superman.
- Me, myself, and I.

Starting to feel a "rhythm" with three things?

- Healthy, wealthy, and wise. - An old saying.
- "Just Do It!" - The Nike slogan.
- Mind, body, and spirit.
- "Three Blind Mice."
- Stop. Look. And listen.

Humans love choices, but not too many choices.

- The Three Musketeers.
- "Friends, Romans, Countrymen."
- "I came, I saw, I conquered."

- "Blood, sweat, and tears."

We overwhelm our prospects with data. If we keep in mind the "rule of three," we can condense our message and make it easier to remember.

Prove this to ourselves.

Try this in conversation.

"When mom dragged the giant chainsaw into the kitchen, I knew dinner was going to be epic. But there were three things she didn't tell us ..."

And then stop. Wait. And wait.

The listeners can't stand it. They want to know those three things.

Mentioning only three things will tell them this won't take long. They want to know now. They are hooked!

Let's try a few "three things" hooks.

- Three ways to fire our boss.
- Three reasons we should quit our jobs now.
- Three breakfast foods that burn fat.
- Three tax deductions we can use now.
- Three tips to feel like an over-caffeinated teenager.
- Three things that wrinkle our skin faster.
- Three cures for that pot-belly look.
- The three things our boss will never tell us when we get hired.
- How to make our boss cry in three easy steps.

Need more ideas?

- Three things supermodels know about wrinkles.
- Three questions you should ask your boss tomorrow.
- The three-penny migraine remedy from Europe.
- The three words that will terrify your boss.
- Use these three tips to get out of debt.
- Would you rather have a three-day workweek?
- Three questions you must ask before leaving for work every morning.

These are some simple ideas to start. Now we can combine "three things" with other hooks and make them more powerful.

- "My rich neighbor told me, 'There are three ways to fire your boss.'"
- "Of course my family needs my paycheck, but there are three reasons we should quit our jobs now."
- "What can the government do without? My tax money! I just found out three tax deductions we can use now."
- "Growing old really hurts, but I have three tips that make me feel like a million dollars."
- "My mirror told me I was getting old, so my sister told me three things that wrinkle my skin faster."
- "My steering wheel kept poking me, so the mechanic gave me three cures for my pot belly."
- "I got conned. My boss never told me these three downsides to my job."
- "My philosophy? Don't get mad. Get even. This is how we can make our boss cry in three easy steps."

It is easier for our prospects to remember three things. Let's make our three things count.

CUTE, CLEVER, CONFUSING, AND INEFFECTIVE.

These are bad and confusing headlines. Yes, they are funny, but they force our prospects to think too hard. If the joke is too difficult to understand, we fail. We want our prospects' attention, not their confusion.

- "Miners refuse to work after death."
- "Juvenile court to try shooting defendant."
- "Hospitals are sued by 7 foot doctors."
- "Dog for sale. Eats anything and is fond of children."
- "Counting calories is for accountants."

We get the idea. This is our time for business, not social laughs.

Save these types of confusing openings for humorous conversations with friends. A few more?

- "Our goal is to get you into networking, so you can get into not-working."
- "Go from Networking to Not-working."

Definitely a clever use of words, but we can do better.

Remember, when we talk to our prospects, we want clarity. If our prospects have to think too hard to understand our message, their minds give up. They go back to the comfort of their own thoughts.

But if we still want humor, read on.

THE HUMOR HOOK.

Human brains are prediction machines. We try to guess what will happen next. This is our survival program keeping us alive and safe.

And what can make us laugh? Our predictions proving to be totally wrong.

Think about stand-up comedians. They misdirect our expectations with a short story. Our mind thinks ahead for an expected conclusion. And then the comedians surprise us with a funny ending.

Here are some of our favorite examples.

Terry Bechtol says, "My wife and I have many arguments, but she only wins half of them. My mother-in-law wins the other half."

This one by comedian Laura Kightlinger has an effective and unexpected ending. "I can't think of anything worse after a night of drinking than waking up next to someone and not being able to remember their name, or how you met … or why they're dead."

And finally, comedian Joe Wong tells this short story.

"I grew up in a poor neighborhood in China. The middle school decided to pave the dirt roads with bricks of cement. The students were required to bring bricks to school. We worked really hard for three weeks. And finally we built a road."

Some laughter from the audience. Then he continues.

"Years later I heard about the term 'child labor.'" (More laughter. Then ...)

"I was like, 'What? Those kids got paid?'"

We didn't expect that ending, and we laugh.

Okay, these are professional comedians. They practiced for years. Humor isn't easy, but when it works, prospects get hooked into our conversation. The good news is that as amateurs, we don't need 45 minutes of great humor. One or two sentences will fit our needs.

What are more ways to make a situation or story humorous?

Incongruity. This means something doesn't fit, such as a cat at a dog's birthday party. Gary Larson's *The Far Side* comics had animals saying things that humans would normally say.

In movies, after an intense scene of action, many times they add an out-of-place humorous quip. This is done to relieve the tension for the audience.

What is the safest type of humor?

Making fun of our mistakes. Listeners will feel superior, we won't offend them, and we have plenty of mistakes to choose from.

Some examples?

We could start our conversation with, "Genetically we are programmed to conserve energy. To be lazy. But now we have unlimited food. It is so hard to diet."

Yawn. Boring. Sales pitch approaching. True facts, but no hook.

Let's add a little humor.

"I exercised for the last 30 days with zero results. I jumped to conclusions, sneezed vigorously, and jogged my memory. Want to hear my new plan?"

"I got tired of organizing my bills by their overdue dates. I got a plan to pay off everything. Would you like to know my brilliant plan?"

"This morning I told my boss off! Okay, I just complained inside of my head, but this is what I almost said out loud."

"My boss was so glad to get rid of me, he helped me pack my desk right after he fired me."

"My career choices? With my grades, my only chance to get into medical school would be in a test tube. I had to find a better way to get ahead."

"I found out I was a terrible boss, but at least I paid myself well."

"I failed at my original goal of winning the lottery. But this plan seems to be working fine."

"My doctor gasped as he looked at my medical records. He turned to me, and said, 'You have to pay for your medical appointments with cash. No more fast food coupons accepted.'"

Whoa! Yes, this doomsday hook started out with an ominous tone, but with a little humorous unexpected hook at the end.

Humor isn't easy. Some people are born with a great sense of humor and impeccable timing, and others, well, they should stick with other hook techniques.

Humor is personal.

Some prospects find humor watching people belly-flopping into a swimming pool. Others love subtle high-brow humor. One size doesn't fit all, and one joke doesn't fit all either.

How do we know if our humor hooks will have a good chance of success? Test them. Try our humor hooks and watch the reactions. Good comedians test jokes all the time. We can follow their method. Something can be hilarious to us, but we could be the only one who appreciates the humor.

An example of humor on the edge that could fail?

A husband compliments his wife on her youthful looks. He smiles and says, "Hey dear, you haven't changed a bit. You are like a vampire who never ages and stays young forever."

The funeral is scheduled for next week.

Another dark humor opening hook?

"The extra bacon double cheeseburger in my right hand prevented me from clutching my heart."

We've discussed many great hooks already. But we have even more to choose from!

THE CONVERSATION HOOK.

Conversations attract our attention. Humans love to eavesdrop.

Imagine we conduct a group presentation. Whether it is in person, or even by video, our audience must forget their current thoughts. Next, they must concentrate on our message. This will be a huge task for us.

Are we up to the task? Will we open our presentation with a great hook? Or will we miss our opportunity to capture our prospects' attention?

Our audience folds their arms, leans back, and waits to judge us. How can we get them to dismiss their "judging thoughts?" Let's try this.

We start by saying, "Before we started tonight, my mom told me, 'If you are going to talk to …'"

Our group leans in, waiting to hear the rest of our mother's message.

They're hooked.

Why is conversation such an effective hook?

Conversation pulls us into an action scene, just like a movie. We know the conversation must be important. We love to be entertained. So let's continue.

Let's create some examples using Mom.

- My mom warned me about getting a job. She said, "They will own you. You have to surrender 50 weeks of your life every year. And then it gets worse. You …"
- My mom doesn't curse often, but today she told me …
- My mom's worst advice? She told me …
- My mom puked when she saw what I was paying, and told me, "Son, they are taking advantage of your …"

Are we getting some ideas? And Mom is only one person. Think of how many people we can have conversations with. Our prospects want to listen in. Let's do some practical examples, and this time, we'll pick on our boss.

- My boss called me into the office and told me, "I have some good news and bad news. The bad news is that you are fired. The good news is that you have the rest of the day off."
- My boss called me into his office and asked, "Are we working you too hard? You have lost a lot of weight. If it is some secret diet plan, could you tell me what you are doing?"
- My boss tried to hold back his evil laugh. He smirked and said, "You don't get it. You will never get ahead here." I didn't know what to say next.
- I overheard my boss whispering into his phone, "He's here. Now. You tell him."

We can state a fact. Our prospect ignores our fact. But put that fact into a conversation, and presto! Our prospect will pay more attention to our fact. This helps us deliver our message.

Who should we pick on next? Let's try a variety of people.

- My doctor frowned and said, "I don't say this often, but …"
- My teenager screamed, "Mom! Dad! I …"
- I overheard my coworkers gossiping about me. They whispered …
- Bankers don't normally greet us by saying, "This is hard for me to say, but …"
- My daughter's first words made me cry. She said …
- Car salesmen are so rude. My salesman told me …

Who can resist these types of hook openings? Very few.

And who can we pick on next? Us!

We can share the conversations we hold inside our heads.

- I told myself, "I will never pay these outrageous rates! I am switching now."
- I thought, "Is there a better way to make a living? Something that will let me see my family more?"
- I fumed. The manager wouldn't give me a refund. But then remembered, "My legal membership will crush this manager like a grape. I will smile when he begs to give me the refund."
- My inner voice wanted to say what I really thought, but my outer voice only said, "Okay, I will work this weekend too."
- When I looked in the mirror I thought, "That face looks a lot older than I remember."
- I looked at my grandchildren and thought, "Do I want them surrounded by chemicals? After all, we grew up with chemicals and look how bad we turned out."

- I was thinking, "I can't see my belt. I know it is there. I can feel it. But why are all my diets failing me?"

- I looked at her and thought, "How can one person have so much energy? I wonder what is in her coffee."

- My mind felt numb, frozen. And then I asked myself, "Should I go for it? Or give up and stay where I am?"

- I wondered, "Why was my neighbor in a lawn chair instead of going to work?"

Everyone loves conversations.

STORY HOOKS.

Our brains are wired for stories. Our subconscious minds tell us, "Wait! Forget everything. This is a story. It might give us a lesson for our future survival. We can learn from others without experiencing any risk."

Getting our prospects' initial attention is the easy part.

The hard part is keeping their attention when we tell a story. Rambling stories that go on for too long will fail. Social stories can take longer, but our business "hook stories" must get to the point immediately.

Here is an easy formula for our story hooks.

1. We need to specify our timeframe. Did this happen 200 years ago? Will it happen in the future? If we make that clear, our prospects can concentrate on the rest of our story. Some ways to immediately clarify the timing of our story?

- "Once upon a time ..."
- "When I was young ..."
- "Yesterday ..."
- "Last night ..."
- "When you started this company ..."
- "When we decided to get married ..."
- "Imagine you could ..."

2. Who is the story about? There isn't any reason for our prospects to care about our story if there isn't anyone to care about. Let's get that question off our prospects' minds. Some starters:

- "I ..."
- "My boss ..."
- "The mother-in-law ..."
- "My oldest daughter ..."

3. Where did this story take place? In outer space? Our parents' backyard? Prospects need a setting for the story so they can visualize the scene inside their heads.

- "At the taco stand ..."
- "In my basement ..."
- "Over the river ..."
- "In my new car ..."
- "In your office ..."

4. Get into the action as soon as possible. If the main character is doing something or experiencing something, our prospects will want to know what comes next. Don't start with boring background information. That is a deadly mistake. Start with the action. A few examples:

- "Eating pizza."
- "Talking to my boss."
- "Trying to pay my bills."
- "Looking in the mirror."

Introduce these four elements early in our story. This makes us look professional. Here are the elements again:

1. When is this story happening?

2. Who is this story about?

3. Where is this story taking place?

4. What is happening?

Here is the first example.

- "On Saturday, while cleaning out my garage, my daughter …"

We have all four elements of our story before we finish the first sentence! With a little planning, we can make our story hooks awesome. We get to the point and will direct our prospects' attention to what comes next. Ka-ching! Success.

One of the best story openings in marketing? This opening sold over a billion dollars in subscriptions:

"On a beautiful late spring afternoon, twenty-five years ago, two young men graduated from the same college …"

A simple opening hook that works. Our thoughts after reading this? "What happened next?" And we haven't even read the entire sentence!

Dale Carnegie's book, *How to Win Friends and Influence People*, sold over 30 million copies. That is a lot of books. How did he start his book? With a story hook.

"On May 7, 1931, the most sensational manhunt New York City had ever known had come to its climax. After weeks of search, 'Two Gun' Crowley - the killer, the gunman who didn't smoke or drink - was at bay, trapped in his sweetheart's apartment on West End Avenue."

And readers thought, "What happened next?"

We don't have to possess superhuman writing skills. Anyone can start a good story by including these elements.

Are there more skills to creating our own stories? Of course. We can invest years learning writing skills at our local university. But for now, we don't have time. We need to hook our prospects' attention.

Here are more examples of including all four elements. Don't panic if we only include two or three elements. We will improve.

- "Yesterday I found myself struggling with my income tax receipts when …"
- "I didn't believe in vampires, but when I showed up for work on Monday …"
- "Tomorrow, my bank's loan officer will have to apologize for …"
- "While eating at my local donut shop this morning …"
- "While looking at my face in the mirror last night …"

There is a lot packed into those few words. Great story hooks have great starts. Every prospect can keep their focus on our story, at least until the end of our first sentence. We make it easy for them to give us their attention.

Look at the difference.

An amateur says: "I have a benefit. Do you want to hear my commercial?"

A professional says: "I have an interesting story. Do you want to hear how it ends?"

Our team members complain, "No one wants to listen to me." Hmmm. Do we see the problem? Our team members don't have uninterested prospects. Our team members have uninteresting story hooks.

Let's have some fun and do a few more examples. And remember, the more of the four elements we can include, the better.

- "At the family reunion, I wondered why my mother-in-law brought a chainsaw into …"
- "I got a surprise when I opened this morning's messages …"
- "I thought I was on the path to becoming a millionaire, but yesterday …"
- "Tomorrow, you open up your emails at work and …"
- "I didn't mean to make the police officer angry, but she insisted on giving me a ticket for …"
- "When I asked her to marry me, she turned, looked over the cliff …"

A few more to get our brains warmed up?

- "I woke up this morning with a migraine, and I remembered why I shouldn't …"
- "One minute before the big argument, I thought …"
- "Last month I forgot to order …"
- "During breakfast I watched a one-minute commercial …"
- "While stocking up on body fat at the donut shop this morning, I learned …"
- "On Saturday, I was standing in line at the bank and …"
- "When I came back from my vacation, I …"

- "When I saw my bank's service charges on my bill, I immediately ..."

Four little steps. Easy. When we think of what we plan to say for our story hooks, remember:

1. When.

2. Who.

3. Where.

4. What's happening.

So which stories do prospects love most?

Here is the politically correct answer. Prospects love stories where we show our vulnerability.

The reality? People love hearing disaster stories where we made mistakes.

Can people be cruel and enjoy our misfortune? Possibly. But think about the survival programs in our minds. When we hear about someone experiencing a misfortune, we take note. We think, "Yeah. Glad to hear that. Now I know to avoid that mistake. I don't have to experience the pain personally."

Some misfortune story hooks? Let's try a few.

- "When my boss fired me yesterday ..."
- "I tried dieting for a month, but I gained ..."
- "When my grandson asked why my wrinkles were so deep ..."
- "You won't believe the mistake I made today ..."
- "I embarrassed myself again yesterday at work ..."
- "I am so annoyed with myself for ..."

- "I didn't mean to …"
- "Taking this job was only my first mistake …"
- "This morning I thought I was so smart, but when I …"
- "Everyone laughed at me when I …"

Our prospects can't wait to see what happens to us next.

Humility doesn't offend prospects. In fact, when we are humble, their defense mechanisms relax. Everyone hates the braggart who tries to impress.

Trained writers know that starting with an anecdote is a great way to hook readers. Readers want to know how the story will end.

Stories work. They have worked for thousands of years. And the best part?

It is easy for humans to remember stories. Our message will live longer in our prospects' minds.

STATISTICS.

Humans and math are two words that don't belong in the same sentence.

The human brain isn't optimized to create math models. We tend to get bored quickly. Math is a recent discovery in the history of mankind. Our evolving brains might need another hundred thousand years to grasp math in a meaningful way.

- 41% of Americans refuse to answer poll questions.
- Only 15.4% of high school graduates can do basic algebra.
- 4 out of 7 statistics are made up.
- 87% of humans can't scientifically verify information.
- 96% of humans fail to do math statistics in their heads.

Have we zoned out yet?

Then is math useless in our conversations and presentations? A full 91% of readers will get this answer right.

Stories are magnets for our brains. We love stories. But have we noticed that very few stories have the word "math" in their titles?

Should we never use math in our hooks? Generally, the rule is to avoid math. Or, if we need to mention a number, make it a simple number. But don't expect our prospects to process that number in their brains. They will ignore the number and wait for something more interesting.

What is good about statistics and math?

Most people believe statistics are true. Statistics come from science. We assume smart people have checked the accuracy for us. So we accept statistics as true, and we don't ask for proof. Humans are lazy.

For example, we say, "An 11% unemployment rate means we must start our own business."

Our prospects' brains react by thinking, "Yeah. That sounds serious to me. 11%? That seems like a lot. Now, tell me a story."

Maybe we sell a product. We announce, "Our lipid formula is 41% more absorbable than 62.5% of the current products in our health category."

What would our prospects think? "Uh, I guess your product is good. Now, stop that number torture and tell me a story."

Few people will challenge our statistics. It's too much work to investigate math that we don't care about anyway. Who cares if 11.2% or if 13.4% of high school students choose accounting as their university major anyway?

Many network marketers love mentioning their company statistics in their presentations. It doesn't turn out well. Some examples?

What we say: "This program will save you 2,200 hours."

What prospects hear: "The program might save me time."

What we say: "Our proprietary formula has 100 milligrams of magic fairy essence."

What prospects hear: "Magic fairy essence. Sounds good."

What we say: "Our compensation plan pays 4% on level three accumulated volume."

What prospects hear: "Money. Money is good."

What we say: "Our company has been in business since 1984."

What prospects hear: "1984. Yeah. That was a good movie. Great dystopian science fiction."

What we say: "Our moisturizer penetrates all 17 layers of our skin."

What prospects hear: "I wonder if it will get rid of my pimples."

What we say: "Our five-star customer service has a 4.33 average rating."

What prospects hear: "Hmmm. Got any stories? I would like to hear a story."

Bottom line? We might love our statistics, but our prospects don't care.

SHOCKING FACT HOOK.

This one is easy to explain.

If our opening fact shocks, creates interest, or surprises our prospects, we get an audience. Humans love discovery.

Let's do it! Ready?

- I found out why vegans who exercise get so many heart attacks.
- I didn't know that commuting to work takes 2.3 years off our lives.
- It turns out that pimpled high school freshmen have a higher net worth than their parents.
- It seems that 8 out of 10 homes in our neighborhood get ripped off on their utility bills.

This is too easy.

Can't think of any shocking facts? There are plenty of shocking facts on the Internet. The secret is to find shocking facts that align with our business.

- Why mothers have better-looking skin than their daughters.
- Why dieting makes things worse.
- How calling in sick helps us get raises.

It doesn't take much imagination to see where these hooks can lead us. We put our prospects' attention on a path that includes our products, services, and opportunity. Let's do a few more shocking fact hooks.

- Two out of three people are ripped off on their phone bills.
- Cleaning our floors can be as bad for our lungs as smoking.
- The one ingredient in shampoo that hastens hair loss.
- How to lose money in our savings account every month.
- High school students have more net worth than their drowning-in-debt parents.
- Americans spend four times as much on their hair as they spend on their minds.
- In a room of ten Americans, four will retire broke.
- Only 1 out of 10 people hired at this company is still employed 3 years later. Ouch!

Got a great shocking fact for our business? It only takes one. This is a very quick way to get our prospects to say, "Tell me more."

DOOM.

Doom and gloom. We can't look away.

If there is a car accident, the traffic slows down in both directions so we can look. We are morbidly fascinated by disaster.

What about the news? Newsroom editors have a mantra: "If it bleeds, it reads." Media is competitive, so each media outlet tries to bleed even more. If they can captivate (or hook) viewers, they can sell advertising. This is capitalism at work.

Our brain's primary program? Survival. The media triggers this program by showing us:

- Chaos.
- Shocking near-misses.
- Death.
- Epidemics.
- Heart-breaking events.
- Murders.
- Floods.
- Fires.
- Crime.
- Gripping tragedies.
- Violence.

Each emotionally-charged word of the media broadcasts gets our attention.

Are we secretly rejoicing in other people's misfortune? No. We are good people. We wish good things for others. However, we can't turn away from disasters. We drive slowly by car accidents, gawking out our window. Our survival program controls our lives ... and our attention.

Think of our prospects. They train their minds to look for doom. Even the smallest hint of bad news will hook our prospects' attention. Fortunately, we don't have to be subtle. We can be direct.

The doom hook creates a feeling of impending disaster.

Skeptical that this is effective? Then try this.

Walk out of the boss's office and announce to the rest of our fellow office workers, "We are doomed!"

Yeah, we've got their attention. Their brains are screaming, "Go on! Go on! What? Continue!"

Let's take a look at some riveting opening hooks that tell our survival programs to pay attention.

- "I knew my company was going out of business soon."
- "The checking account was empty, but it was only the 23rd of the month."
- "I arrived home and the garage was empty."
- "I could see the wrinkles growing on my forehead."

What response can we expect from our prospects? They want to know what happens next. They can't wait to observe disaster.

Does this mean we should focus on the negative, and not the positive? Well, the media tested positive news versus negative news. Which grabs attention better? Negative news.

Compare these two opening hooks:

Headline #1: "Mother loves daughter and teaches her better study habits."

Headline #2: "Mother disowns daughter over homework failure."

Doom sells.

Add tension.

We love stories. And what makes a good story? Tension. We're afraid of what's coming next.

Our story can start calmly, but it will only take a few words to ratchet up the tension and capture our prospects' attention. For example:

"My boss walked into the main office with a box of yellow stickers."

This sentence creates mild curiosity. Listeners want to know about the yellow stickers.

But what if we added just a few more words?

"My boss walked into the main office with a box of yellow stickers that said, 'You are fired!'"

Do we want to know what happens next? Of course. We can't wait for this story to unfold.

We can take a simple fact, and upgrade that fact to a hook of impending doom. Let's try one.

- I am at work.

Definitely a fact. Not very interesting for our listeners. Let's upgrade a little. Here are some suggestions.

- I am struggling at work.
- The tension at work finally exploded.
- One by one, they left the boss's office crying.
- I sat at my desk wondering, "Is this my last paycheck?"
- A note on everyone's desk announced, "Paychecks are delayed."
- I knew my job was in trouble when the police handcuffed and escorted my boss out the front door.

Get the feeling that more bad things are in the future? Prospects want to know what will happen next. Let's continue.

- I arrived at work, but the parking lot was empty.
- The supervisor held pink slips in his hands.
- The 40% pay cut was going to hurt.
- Not even the bosses were spared. We all lost our jobs.
- I could smell that something was wrong at work today.

Gee. Things can't get much worse, or can they?

- The moving company was collecting the furniture when I arrived at work Monday morning.
- Work from home? Ha! Now I have to start my day at 5 am answering emails.
- The only good thing about going out of business is that my stupid boss loses his job too.
- It was 5 pm at work, and everyone was afraid to leave.
- The day before our annual bonuses were supposed to arrive, everyone got a memo to attend a special all-company meeting in the warehouse. No one was smiling.

A few words can make a huge difference. This could be the difference between a new member on our team, or someone who ignores what we're offering.

So much for opportunity. Can we use doom hooks for our product and services? Why not?

- I could feel the pimples working their way to my chin.

- I couldn't hide the growling noise from my stomach.

- The odor from my laundry detergent gave me a headache. I wondered what else it was doing to my brain cells.

- I gained five pounds. My body punished me for trying to diet.

- Why did our neighbors pay less for the same electricity?

There is an old saying, "Bad news travels fast."

Doom sells.

A HOOK CASE STUDY.

Imagine we are overweight. (Some of us can imagine this better than others.)

John, a network marketer selling diet products, approaches us. What are we going to do?

Prejudge him, of course!

- That greedy gleam in his eyes.
- The aroma of unwashed salesman.
- The nervous clearing of his throat.
- The ceremonial application of a closing essential oil.
- The beads of sweat turning into a river.

As John approaches us, we read his mind. He thinks, "Commission!"

We hear a quick, "Hi. How are you?"

And then immediately after, "Lose 10 pounds in 10 days with our diarrhea tea!"

Our reaction?

We go back to eating our French fries and gravy.

This was a failed approach for John. The conversation stops cold.

Now, John did lead with a benefit. A strong benefit. But it wasn't enough. The conversation stopped before he could describe the magic herbs, the guarantee, and the genius scientist who discovered the secret tea leaves.

What was John missing?

A hook.

We have to get our prospects' interest first. That is what the pros do. We want our prospects to engage and ask us to continue. Parroting boring benefits about our company's products or opportunity can work, but the rejection rate is high.

Benefits are great, especially for a friendly audience. But that is what John is missing: a friendly audience. He needs to attract our interest.

Let's look at some ways this conversation could go better. After the obligatory greeting, John's first sentence is:

"Out of hundreds of diets, can you guess which one gets the best results?"

Now we are interested. The hook grabs our curiosity.

We guess, "Only eat standing naked in front of a mirror ... in department stores?"

John smiles, "Nice try. That is good. But science verified that getting a divorce is the #1 most effective weight loss program. People want to look good when they become single. I never would have guessed it either."

Whoa! This is interesting. This answer was not expected. We are hooked. And now John has a friendly audience.

John continues, "Can you guess the second best diet? It is the magic tea diet. Everyone agrees drinking tea is easier than exercising."

Which version of John will make more sales?

1. Amateur John who only recites benefits?

2. Professional John who uses a strong 'unexpected' hook?

It doesn't take a rocket scientist to figure out that Professional John grows his business, while Amateur John struggles.

In this example, Professional John uses a "question hook" plus an "unexpected hook" to grab our interest.

Amateur John has no audience. He gets paid amateur commissions and bonuses.

We don't need a huge inventory of hooks. A few hooks can take us from amateur to professional status.

You might be thinking, "But I don't feel creative!"

Welcome to being ordinary. Thankfully, we can get the inspiration we need from the media. Smart people constantly come up with interesting headlines that can give us ideas for better hooks.

Let's continue the diet example. But remember, we can adjust for any product, service, or opportunity. Just let the media headlines inspire us.

The original headline: "Willpower in a bottle."

Our inspired hook: "My skinny friends never told me that you can buy diet willpower in a bottle."

The original headline: "How to lose weight while watching TV."

Our inspired hook: "My aunt told me how she loses weight while watching late-night TV."

The original headline: "If you don't have time to exercise, this is the diet for you."

Our inspired hook: "Can you guess the 45-second exercise that kickstarts our fat-burning programs?"

The original headline: "Three diet shortcuts that doctors won't tell you."

Our inspired hook: "My doctor told me that most diets are scams. Here are the three diets that work."

The original headline: "Three miracle exercises that reduce cellulite."

Our inspired hook: "I overheard my nieces whisper, 'Cottage cheese thighs.' I knew it was time to find a diet that works."

Now, after doing a few of these, we have our minds working in the right direction. We won't need headlines to inspire us.

Unleash the opening hooks!

- "I now have 17 ice cream recipes that help me lose weight. Maybe I should open a franchise."
- "I did the dumb people diet for six months. No wonder I couldn't lose weight."
- "How many seconds does it take to put our bodies into fat-burning mode?"
- "My surgeon neighbor performed 300 liposuction operations last year. He warned me not to be his next patient, and told me three things I should do."
- "My new diet comes with a catch: I have to like chocolate."
- "Can you guess the three best fat-burning foods?"
- "They gave me a warning. They said if I lose weight too fast, I should eat more ice cream for dessert."

Remember, we can use media headlines to inspire us for any product, service, or opportunity. No need to use the "I am not creative" excuse.

Enough with the product examples.

Let's talk services!

- "My electricity bill is so small, I need a magnifying glass."
- "I wondered, 'What are all these discounts and credits on my bill?'"
- "Why didn't someone tell us that legal services can be so cheap?"
- "Pick a number. Guess how many criminals have all your credit card records already?"
- "I found out how to lower all those credit card fees they charge merchants."
- "Did you get your phone bill reduced by changing your service, too?"

How about opportunity?

- "Did you know that being rich makes us more popular?"
- "I found a get-rich plan that works for people over 40."
- "I found out how others get paid every week, even if they don't show up for work."
- "The winner of the rat race was finally declared. Guess who it is?"

A few more short headline-type hooks?

- "Wave good-bye to your neighbors!"
- "Do you know anyone in pain?"
- "How many pounds overweight should you be at age 50?"
- "Stop. Don't go to work today."
- "I used to have wrinkles ..."

Do we notice anything in these headline hooks?

They are short. Why? Because our prospects have short attention spans, just like we do. Can longer headline hooks work too? Yes, as long as they're good!

With so many hook examples to work with, we will never worry about creating an attentive audience again.

Hooks can change our lives.

"What makes you think I want to hear a sales pitch from you?" There was an ominous tone in the prospect's voice.

Instant rejection. Another failure.

Our distributor licks his wounds over a sad cup of coffee. Looks like he will live to die another day. At this rate, that day will be arriving soon. Full-on depression was kicking in.

And then the blaming began.

"It is not my fault! The top pros won't tell me the secret. Do they think I'm not ready for it??? Well, today I am ready! Bring on the secret!"

Across the table, the Spirit of Skills appears. "You summoned me? Are you ready to upgrade your skills?"

The distributor mumbles, "I thought you would be ... bigger. More impressive. But yeah, I am ready for the secret. And aren't you a little young for a ghost? You should consider getting a few wrinkles and learning to scowl."

The Spirit of Skills smiles. "Nice. Thankfully, if you use the secret, even your acidic social skills won't hold you back. When you are ready to learn, then it will be your time."

The Spirit of Skills begins to fade away.

"Wait! Wait! Don't go. I didn't mean you were too young or immature. Come back! I need the secret. I want the top secret the big earners use for unlimited prospects who beg for presentations."

And that is how our distributor's journey to success began. One invisible sales superpower secret... and everything changed immediately.

The secret?

Hooks! Special words and phrases that compel our prospects to say, "Hey! Let's talk now!"

If we take the time, we can create better hooks. Look for inspiration and then see if our new hook creations have possibilities. Here are a few more hooks to inspire us.

- My 6-year-old knows more than my CPA.
- As I was checking my dog's bank book ...
- My sixth-grader sighed and said, "I need a better side hustle."
- Eleven people wore clown suits at our weekly entrepreneur meeting.
- There are a thousand places to get fired, but a children's petting zoo?

Need more hooks? Let's continue.

THE QUIZ HOOK.

Humans have a quiz addiction. Why?

We want to see how we measure up to our fellow humans. We like to see how smart we are.

Here are three quick rules for maximum quiz engagement:

#1. Promise the quiz will be short. (Humans have short attention spans.)

#2. Personality assessment quizzes are irresistible. (We are insanely curious about personalities. This explains why characters in movies hold our attention.)

#3. End with a challenge. (Get prospects to engage.)

Examples of using these three rules?

- Most people can't pass this five-question health quiz, but I would love to see you try.

- Take this one-minute emotional maturity quiz. Can you score better than your children?

- Test your IQ in two minutes. Will you score better than average?

- Nine signs that your boss is a closet vampire. Does your boss show these signs?

- Which cartoon character does your spouse resemble? Take the test.

- The top five bills you are overpaying. Can you pick them out from this list?

- The seven deadly sins of winning. Do you have them all?

- Can you guess which of these four signs predicts that you will die early?

- Most people can't pass this emotional quiz, but I would love to see your results.

A quiz commands involvement. Our prospects engage with our message instead of ignoring our sales pitch.

Can't think of a good quiz topic?

Try these questions to prompt our creativity.

- How hard will it be for me to … (Stop eating between meals, watching hours of television, find a job I love, learn how to sell, etc.)

- How often do I … (Diet, pay bills, wonder about the future, wake up tired, feel ripped off, worry about my finances, etc.)

- Can I name the four best …(Excuses to show up to work late, vegetables to lose weight, ways to keep skin young, places to save money immediately, tax deductions we aren't using now, etc.)

- How much time does the average person spend … (On social media, sleeping, commuting, etc.)

- How many days can I go without … (Taco Bell, KFC, donuts, etc.)

- Which cartoon character describes … (My financial retirement plan, my personality, my social life, self-discipline, etc.)

Make our quiz worthwhile.

Think about the benefits we wish to highlight. Then, design the best quiz to hook the interest of our ideal prospects.

Is a quiz on the different types of jelly donuts a good way to attract dieters for our diet products? No.

The regulars at the local donut shop won't be interested in our diet products. Yes, they could get a perfect score on the jelly donut quiz. But, our ideal prospects are people who care about their health. Maybe we should have a quiz asking which exercise trims our stomach. More exercise enthusiasts will have an interest. They are a better market for our diet products.

When we can describe our ideal prospect, the subject of our quiz becomes more obvious. Here are a few ideas.

- If we sell skincare products, a quiz about what makes our skin wrinkle.

- If we sell nutritional products, a quiz that estimates our "body age" based upon our lifestyle.

- If we sell phone service or utilities, a quiz about how a little savings can propel us to wealth.

- If we sell our opportunity, a quiz covering the top ten things people hate about their jobs.

Our quiz will get prospects involved. With a little planning, our quiz can highlight their current problems and motivate them to look for solutions.

And finally …

Q. Which type of quiz gets the most interest and engagement?

A. Personality quizzes.

Why? Think about human nature. When visiting with friends, what do people talk about the most? Other people. Gossip.

This should remind us that our quizzes shouldn't be just data, but they should include human feelings. Humans make decisions based upon emotion, and later justify their decisions with logic.

THE CHALLENGE HOOK!

Remember the "ice bucket" challenge? It was one of the most viral campaigns ever. After we dumped a bucket of ice water on ourselves, we challenged our friends to do it. We love challenges, and we enjoy the feeling of being part of a group.

To get more participation in challenges, here are some general guidelines.

1. If the challenge is too difficult, few will participate. Make it easy to do.

2. The shorter the better. Humans don't have good long-term motivation. The future seems too far away.

3. Make the challenge interesting. Humans love to be entertained.

4. We want to "hook" the ideal prospects for our business.

We can create our own challenge. Let's look at some ideas to spark our creativity.

Do you sell skincare? How about a seven-day challenge? Use the regular skincare product on one half of our face, and the new and improved magic skincare product on the other half. Take a picture of our results in seven days.

Some people may not want to participate. No one wants to look like they only aged on one side of their face. But maybe we can get them to do the challenge on their hands? Or arms? Or legs? People want to see a difference.

We don't have to make a claim. We don't have to compare our product with any other product. All we have to do is to get them to try for themselves.

60 years ago, a famous haircare company advertised their product. One ping-pong player used their product and his hair stayed in place during a difficult match. His opponent didn't use their product, and his hair was a mess. They didn't even compare the results to other hair products; they didn't compare to anything! But no one cared. They purchased this wonderful hair product.

What can we compare our products with to highlight how effective they are?

- Does our organic cleaner work better than simple water?
- Does our diet shake work better than the normal fast food meal?
- Is our part-time income better than no part-time income?
- Does our discount travel plan work better than a full-price travel plan?
- Does our energy protein shake in the morning work better than donuts?
- Does saving money on our utilities increase our bank account balance better than if we paid full-price?

It is easy for us to look good with no competition.

We can do challenges with our team members, too.

The competition can be with ourselves, or against others. Some ideas?

- The "call three people every day" challenge.

- The "post our goals" challenge.

- The "make new friends" challenge.

- The "no television" challenge.

- The "give away samples" challenge.

- The "bring a guest" challenge.

Remember, the shorter the challenge, the better. It is easier to keep up our motivation and focus for five days than for 50 days.

Get prospects to join the challenge.

Now for a call-to-action hook. Our prospects are naturally competitive. They love to challenge themselves and compare their results with others.

A simple sentence at the end of our challenge offer can increase our results. Some examples.

- Most people can't score more than five.

- Can you beat the average score of an 11-year-old?

- How many days before you see the difference?

- When you finish, post your score for others to see.

- Can you answer these five questions?

- Only smart people can do this correctly.

Imagine we sell concentrated fruit tablets. Let's put together a challenge that will attract prospects who want better health.

• • •

The seven-day fruit challenge.

Eat two fruit servings at each meal—breakfast, lunch and dinner—for seven days. Post pictures of your meals. Can you do this for seven days?

• • •

Let's review:

- Is this simple?
- Can almost anyone participate?
- Seven days isn't too long.
- It's interesting to see pictures of what the other challenge participants eat.
- Do we feel challenged to do this?

The people participating in the challenge are great prospects for our fruit tablets. We can let them know that eating our concentrated fruit tablets is easier than trying to fit in all that fruit every day. As an added benefit, maybe our fruit tablets will be less expensive, too.

Need a few more ideas?

If we sell discounted services, challenge them to try to get discounts on their current bills. Or challenge them to save money on their groceries. This would pre-sell their minds for our service savings.

If we sell our opportunity, challenge them to get a 5% raise from their boss. Most won't try. They don't want to risk their job security. Now, we are their only solution.

This gets easier in time. Our first idea may not be great, but we don't have to implement our idea yet. Let it sit in our minds for a week. See what other modifications or possibilities we think of. Then, share our idea with a friend. Outside feedback and ideas are always welcomed.

One warning.

Make our challenges based upon the activity, not the result. Why?

We can't control the result. This can discourage participation. An example?

We start a "how many people can we sponsor in a month" challenge. Here is the problem. No matter how hard we work, we can't guarantee that it will be the right time for our prospects to join. That is outside of our control.

Instead, let's start a "how many people can I talk to in a month" challenge. Approaching people and talking to them is within our control. We determine our results. Now anyone can enjoy this challenge.

And finally.

Challenges are fun. When everyone participates, we build a community spirit that makes our challenge more powerful.

Challenges guarantee us space in our prospects' minds. They are great tools for our skill toolbox.

PRESENTATION HOOKS.

Hooks, especially hooks in our first sentence, make us interesting. But what if we included hooks throughout our presentation? What would happen?

Our prospects would love it!

We would love it, too. Why? Because we could keep our prospects' attention for our entire message. Whenever our prospects' minds begin to drift, bang! Another hook. We won't let our prospects' attention wander away, never to return.

How does our competition present their message? Poorly. They watch their presentations unravel with their ancient, moldy skills from the 1970s. They lose their prospects' attention in seconds. PowerPoint slide after PowerPoint slide sends their prospects' attention careening down a cliff, never to be seen again.

If we make our presentation engaging and interesting, we will see our competition fading away in our rearview mirror. It doesn't take much to improve the standard presentation. We will look better with even minor improvements.

Let's look at the standard boring presentations.

These presentations use dull PowerPoint slides, company fluff videos with boring voice-overs, mind-boggling mountains of facts, statistics, and … this is looking ugly.

It gets worse. These presentations forget about our prospects' points of view. The facts are there, but these facts may not be what our prospects are most interested in.

What is our prospect's point of view? "Why am I here? Why do I care? What is in it for me? How does this apply to my situation? Can I picture myself doing this?"

Notice that our prospects are not asking for more proof or facts. Our prospects want to know how all of this applies to their lives.

Let's see the difference now.

The standard boring, fact-filled nutritional company presentation.

"We are the Wonderful Company, located in Wonderful, America. Our founder, Mr. Wonderful, started the Wonderful Company in the wonderful year of 1990. He had a burning desire to search for the secret 'Fountain of Youth.'

"Mr. Wonderful grew up in a log cabin, excelled in school, and is a wonderful family man. After years of boring work for other corporations, Mr. Wonderful took his vision of changing the world to the health industry. He wanted to revolutionize the vitamin and supplement industry with his unique approach to nutrition. His research led him to discover the magic peptide rotating-enzyme molecule."

<Picture our prospects now. Checking their phones for messages, thinking of the funny cat videos they watched that morning. Rolling their eyes in boredom. Yes, Mr. Wonderful has a wonderful life, but that isn't relevant to them. They only worry about themselves. Selfish prospects!>

"This single molecule has the power to make many ordinary harmful synthetic drugs obsolete. To avoid pharmaceutical suppression, Mr. Wonderful created a special direct-to-the-public distribution model. And instead of advertising, he chose the network marketing model of word-of-mouth reimbursement to promote this wonder product."

<Some prospects yawn. Others plot revenge against the friends who invited them to this presentation. But it gets worse.>

"Our state-of-the-art compensation plan pays 41% more on the commissionable point value of each of our premium pro-ducts, and a full 43% more on the commissionable point value of ..."

Did that sound familiar?

Relax. This is what our competition is doing, not us. As we can see, our competition is pathetic. Their presentations are ineffective and antisocial. Their presentations are so bad that no one wants to invite prospects to hear them.

No presentations means no one hears our message. Ouch.

So how many things went wrong with this presentation? Here are a few.

#1. The opening hook? Totally missing. We want a strong opening to tear our prospects' attention away from their other distractions.

#2. Did this presentation feel personal? No. This presentation feels like it came from a soulless corporate office worker reading from a spreadsheet.

#3. Numbers and statistics. Who can visualize the difference between 43% and 41%? No human can do this.

#4. Corporate speak and industry jargon. The audience has no idea what "point value" means.

#5. Boring. Regurgitating facts uses up valuable oxygen. Our audience doesn't need us to read facts to them.

#6. This presentation talked all about the company and what was important to the company. Very little of the presentation pertained to the audience.

We can list more things wrong here, but we want to move on to the positive. Let's see an improved version of a presentation using some hooks.

THE IMPROVED PRESENTATION WITH HOOKS.

Let's use services for this example. Phone plans. Gas and electricity. Legal plans. Merchant services. Credit protection. Oh my, the list can go on and on. But we need to focus on one of these services for our example presentation. Let's choose phone plans.

And let's try to see things from our prospects' points of view as we go through this presentation.

• • •

A more personal presentation for phone plans.

How many people do you know who don't have a phone? Hard to think of someone, isn't it? Even most teenagers have their own phones.

Let's ask ourselves a few questions.

Q. What percentage of people have to pay for their plans?

A. Almost everyone. The phone companies don't like giving people free service.

Here is the next question.

Q. Which is better: A bigger monthly bill, or a smaller monthly bill?

A. Smaller. We can use the money we save to do something fun.

The last question?

> Q. Most people don't know that they can pay less. If we told them they have the option for a lower phone bill, would they at least appreciate that we let them know?

> A. Most people would thank us for letting them know.

And that is what we do. If you like helping people, by letting them know they have an option to pay less, this is a great business for you. You can make a difference in other people's lives.

And this gets better.

Every month when they enjoy their lower phone bill, we get paid. Yes, we get paid because we improve other people's lives. The more people we help, the more we make.

Imagine getting an extra paycheck every month for helping others save money. When I check my bank balance every month, I get excited. I can't wait to see how much money the company adds to my account, just because I let others know they could pay less. It sort of feels like Christmas 12 times a year. We are using the extra money to pay off our home and to take nicer holidays.

But I know what you are thinking. You're wondering, "That sounds good. A part-time income would definitely help. But I would love to do this for a full-time career. Is it possible to earn enough to replace my job? Could I even exceed my current income?"

Yes, of course. That's basic math. If we help a lot of people save money, we will earn a lot more. But here is some good news.

You and I are not alone. We know others that could use an extra paycheck every month, too. Let's encourage them to help others save money on their phone bills. They will also get extra money every month. They will thank us for the opportunity.

And when they help others save money, we get credit for that work, too. This helps us earn faster. Now our dream of a full-time career working from home gets closer. We can go as slow or as fast as we want.

Here is the bottom line. We have choices:

#1. We can continue to pay more for our phone service, or we can choose to pay less. This is an easy choice. After all, we have math skills.

#2. We can choose to let others know they can save money. It is up to them, but most people will want the savings. If we let others know, we can count on extra money in our bank account every month. We can choose to let others know and get paid. Or we could choose to keep this top-secret, and let them suffer because no one told them. This is an easy choice for most of us.

#3. We can choose to make this a full-time career if we want. We will have to work harder to get there, but for many of us, this could be a dream come true.

So let me end with some good news and some bad news.

The bad news is that so many people don't know about these options.

The good news is that we do.

Here is our chance to make some choices for our lives.

● ● ●

Done.

Did we notice any hooks in this presentation?

Of course. The difference is obvious. With even minimal effort, we can improve the standard "read some PowerPoint slides" presentation.

Can we use this template for skincare? Yes. For diet products? Yes. For natural cleaning products? Yes. For legal services? Yes.

So what is holding us back from introducing more hooks at the beginning, middle, and end of our presentation? Nothing. We can improve now.

LIFE WITHOUT HOOKS.

Not too long ago, a stranger sent this message to me on social media. (It's been slightly edited to protect me from the sender's wrath, in case he reads this.)

• • •

Hello.

Did you know that as you age, your brain cells deteriorate? By age 35 you only have 50% of your thinking power, and by age 65 you have almost none left. Your short-term memory will barely work.

The weaker your brain cells are, the faster you will age, and the slower you will heal.

Now, thanks to an affordable and historic breakthrough in brain cell regeneration technology, you can revive your own brain cells without painful and expensive injections.

You can feel energetic, think clearly, and live longer with your younger brain.

And this costs less than two pizza slices a day!

I have a three-minute video that covers the details. If I sent you the link, would you watch it?

If yes, reply with "Thumbs Up."

Thanks.

Signed, John "No Hooks" Smith

• • •

I almost rolled my eyes out of my head after reading this message.

How can one networker pack so many mistakes into one little message? I couldn't respond. Why? Because I am over 65 and have no brain cells left!

It might take years of psychotherapy to remove this painful memory.

This message illustrates how good hooks can save our network marketing career. Instead of pitching and selling, we can attract volunteers who beg us to tell them more.

But my pain didn't end with this first message. More grief was on its way.

Message #2.

• • •

A networker said: "Hi! Random question, sort of out of the blue, but do you take collagen?"

I said: "That is pretty random. Yes, I take collagen."

The networker said: "That's great! Do you like taking it? Have you noticed a difference since you started!"

I said: "Uh, why do you ask?" (This isn't passing the smell test. An ominous cloud of skepticism forms in my brain. Wait for it! Wait for it! I know the sales pitch is coming.)

The networker said: "My company just launched a new micro-crystalized extracted bio-enhanced collagen product. They are looking for more testimonials. I'm trying it out for the next month. I've got the hookup for a 30-day risk free trial with over 40% off. Want to give it a shot with me?"

(I know the networker meant well. Maybe he had just finished listening to an over-hyped motivational speech. I tried to say "no" without hurting his feelings.)

> **I said:** I am sure your company has enough testimonials. Here is a little PDF guide on how to market nutritionals. Hope your team enjoys it.

> **The networker said:** "That's nice of you to send. Thank you. I asked you specifically, as a person, if you'd consider trying it because ours is the most nutritionally-sound, absorption-enhanced, bioavailable elixir on the market. It's marine type 1 and has been showing incredible results. If I sent you a three-minute video, would you watch it?"

• • •

Oh my. Maybe this second networker is a long-lost twin of the first networker. Both messages are one-way communication. This isn't going to end well. My day is ruined after only two messages.

We can do better than this.

If these two sample messages represent our competition, our hooks should make us superstars. Most networkers don't even bother with hooks. They prefer to dump data on their unsuspecting prospects.

What about us? We will use a great hook in our opening to capture our prospects' attention. We won't wait until the ten-minute mark in our conversations to do this. That is too late.

And rather than using random oral diarrhea for our opening conversations with prospects, we will use our hook skills to get an eager audience for our message. This puts us ahead of everyone.

Enjoy creating great hooks to attract your prospects' interest!

Thank you.

Thank you for purchasing and reading this book. We hope you found some ideas that will work for you.

Before you go, would it be okay if we asked a small favor? Would you take just one minute and leave a sentence or two reviewing this book online? Your review can help others choose what they will read next. It would be greatly appreciated by many fellow readers.

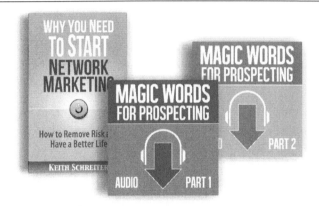

More Books from Big Al Books
BigAlBooks.com

Mindset Series

Secrets to Mastering Your Mindset
Take Control of Your Network Marketing Career

Breaking the Brain Code
Easy Lessons for Your Network Marketing Career

How to Get Motivated in 60 Seconds
The Secrets to Instant Action

Prospecting and Recruiting Series

How to Get Appointments Without Rejection
Fill Our Calendars with Network Marketing Prospects

Create Influence
10 Ways to Impress and Guide Others

How to Meet New People Guidebook
Overcome Fear and Connect Now

How to Get Your Prospect's Attention and Keep It!
Magic Phrases for Network Marketing

10 Shortcuts Into Our Prospects' Minds
Get Network Marketing Decisions Fast!

How To Prospect, Sell And Build Your Network Marketing Business With Stories

26 Instant Marketing Ideas To Build Your Network Marketing Business

51 Ways and Places to Sponsor New Distributors
Discover Hot Prospects For Your Network Marketing Business

First Sentences for Network Marketing
How To Quickly Get Prospects On Your Side

Big Al's MLM Sponsoring Magic
How To Build A Network Marketing Team Quickly

Start SuperNetworking!
5 Simple Steps to Creating Your Own Personal Networking Group

Getting Started Series

How to Build Your Network Marketing Business in 15 Minutes a Day

3 Easy Habits For Network Marketing
Automate Your MLM Success

Quick Start Guide for Network Marketing
Get Started FAST, Rejection-FREE!

Core Skills Series

How To Get Instant Trust, Belief, Influence and Rapport!
13 Ways To Create Open Minds By Talking To The
Subconscious Mind

Ice Breakers!
How To Get Any Prospect To Beg You For A Presentation

Pre-Closing for Network Marketing
"Yes" Decisions Before The Presentation

The Two-Minute Story for Network Marketing
Create the Big-Picture Story That Sticks!

Personality Training Series (The Colors)

The Four Color Personalities for MLM
The Secret Language for Network Marketing

Mini-Scripts for the Four Color Personalities
How to Talk to our Network Marketing Prospects

Why Are My Goals Not Working?
Color Personalities for Network Marketing Success

How To Get Kids To Say Yes!
Using the Secret Four Color Languages to Get Kids to Listen

Presentation and Closing Series

Closing for Network Marketing
Getting Prospects Across The Finish Line

The One-Minute Presentation
Explain Your Network Marketing Business Like A Pro

How to Follow Up With Your Network Marketing Prospects
Turn Not Now Into Right Now!

Retail Sales for Network Marketers
How to Get New Customers for Your MLM Business

Leadership Series

The Complete Three-Book Network Marketing Leadership Series
Series includes: How To Build Network Marketing Leaders Volume One, How To Build Network Marketing Leaders Volume Two, and Motivation. Action. Results.

How To Build Network Marketing Leaders
Volume One: Step-By-Step Creation Of MLM Professionals

How To Build Network Marketing Leaders
Volume Two: Activities And Lessons For MLM Leaders

Motivation. Action. Results.
How Network Marketing Leaders Move Their Teams

What Smart Sponsors Do
Supercharge Our Network Marketing Team

More Books...

Why You Need to Start Network Marketing
How to Remove Risk and Have a Better Life

How To Build Your Network Marketing Nutrition Business Fast

How Speakers, Trainers, and Coaches Get More Bookings
12 Ways to Flood Our Calendars with Paid Events

How To Build Your Network Marketing Utilities Business Fast

Getting "Yes" Decisions
What insurance agents and financial advisors can say to clients

Public Speaking Magic
Success and Confidence in the First 20 Seconds

Worthless Sponsor Jokes
Network Marketing Humor

About the Authors

Keith Schreiter has 20+ years of experience in network marketing and MLM. He shows network marketers how to use simple systems to build a stable and growing business.

So, do you need more prospects? Do you need your prospects to commit instead of stalling? Want to know how to engage and keep your group active? If these are the types of skills you would like to master, you will enjoy his "how-to" style.

Keith speaks and trains in the U.S., Canada, and Europe.

Tom "Big Al" Schreiter has 40+ years of experience in network marketing and MLM. As the author of the original "Big Al" training books in the late '70s, he has continued to speak in over 80 countries on using the exact words and phrases to get prospects to open up their minds and say "YES."

His passion is marketing ideas, marketing campaigns, and how to speak to the subconscious mind in simplified, practical ways. He is always looking for case studies of incredible marketing campaigns that give usable lessons.

As the author of numerous audio trainings, Tom is a favorite speaker at company conventions and regional events.

Printed in Poland
by Amazon Fulfillment
Poland Sp. z o.o., Wrocław